The Mindset of a Gentleman

10 Success Principles to Motivate, Inspire & Increase Your Productivity

RL Taylor

The Midset of a Gentleman
Copyright 2017 by RL Taylor

The information contained within this book is strictly for educational purposes. If you wish to apply ideas contained in this book, you are taking full responsibility for your actions.

The author has made every effort to ensure the accuracy of the information within this book was correct at time of publication. The author does not assume and hereby disclaims any liability to any party for any loss, damage, or disruption caused by errors or omissions, whether such errors or omissions result from accident, negligence, or any other cause.

Published in Michigan by Another Clue Publishing.

To order additional or bulk copies of this book please contact@ harrisonblakeapparel.com

ISBN 978-0692829301

For my children
SA & HB

Always follow your dreams.
Use your creativity…
You can do anything!

TABLE OF CONTENTS

INTRODUCTION

❧

As I embark on this new literary journey I find myself in an unusual position. Just a few days before beginning to write this I was taking a motorcycle class. There I was trying to learn something new when in the blink of an eye things changed.

One moment I was making a routine left turn and the next moment I was looking up at the drizzling rain dripping from gray clouds overhead, wondering what happened. I did my best tough guy act, hopped up, shook myself off and tried to gather myself, but something was noticeably wrong. My shoulder felt strange. An ambulance was ushered onto the scene and I was whisked away to a local hospital.

We'll revisit the story later on and you'll learn exactly how I fared and why it means anything as far as this book is concerned.

I've been wanting to get back into writing for a while now. There's a few reasons. It's quite therapeutic and relaxing. I love writing and I love helping people. My last book, *The Life of a Gentleman,* has changed some lives. It is a guide to assist men in living as true gentlemen. With this effort, I wanted to dive deeper, if you will.

Let's look at the root of it all. The exterior can be polished, but the inside can be a complete mess. That is true with automobiles as well as with people.

If we capture the correct mindset needed, we can execute all the external maneuvers necessary to prove ourselves worthy of the title, Gentleman.

I've put off this book for long enough. Honestly, I've been thinking about writing it for quite some time. I've had the thoughts in my head, but I haven't put pen to paper. But now things have changed. It's been about three years since my last effort to produce a book. Needless to say, it's time.

I remember writing *The Life of a Gentleman* and thinking to myself that the book had the potential to impact so many people and I hope that it did serve its purpose. But the thing is, in just this brief period of time so much has changed in our society.

In *The Life of a Gentleman* I spoke about how one could gain more respect and etiquette by presenting themselves as a gentleman. Sadly, when we look at society today, sometimes your appearance and how you present yourself ends up mattering little or not enough. So this time around I thought I would tackle the subject of a gentleman from a different angle.

Being a gentleman means different things to different people, but it still has meaning. It's a mindset and that's why this book will be titled *The Mindset of a Gentleman*.

Your mind is the one thing no one can strip away from you. No one can get inside your head and tell you how to feel about yourself. From my research this is the most important aspect of living the life of a gentleman, because if you believe in yourself it will be noticeable to others. Your true self-worth will be undeniable to all onlookers.

I could go on and give tutorials about how to shine your shoes or how to make sure your clothes fit properly, but what would that accomplish? I'm not saying those skills are of no importance. They are valuable skills. Yes, of course those things are important, but even of more importance is your mindset. Your mindset will prepare you to face obstacles and challenges that will arise. Emphasis should be placed on when and not if.

Being a gentleman is more than just dressing nice and having good manners. This standard of living totally encompasses your entire life. As we all know life is complicated and full of curveballs and difficulties.

The way that we handle those inconveniences can be altered by our mindset. This is one of my principle reasons for thinking this book will be of great benefit to you. This is the next logical step to living the life of a gentleman.

By the conclusion of this book you will have read many real life experiences. Hopefully you will have learned many techniques and principles that will assist you in living the best way possible. When you think of a gentleman you think of someone poised, someone calm, well-equipped to handle the many challenges that life hurls their way on a repeated basis.

How does one master these abilities? How does one become equipped to handle the stress? Are you ready to find out? I certainly invite you to answer with a resounding yes. Let's take this journey together!

HOPE THE EXPERIENCE

∞

"Hope is being able to see that there is light despite all of the darkness"

- Desmond Tutu

In 1989 I was a young man going on a fishing trip with my father. We lived in New England and we often headed to the coast for a trip out on the ocean for a chartered fishing experience. I still remember waking up before dawn, loading up the truck and hitting the road while the rest of the world was sleep. The cool air breezing through the windows, stars still in the sky as we drove towards our adventure.

My father had a friend joining us on this trip and I too had a buddy tagging along to keep me company on the trip. We'd chartered a private boat with a weathered and experienced fisherman who was going to take us out deep into saltwater on the Atlantic Ocean and I couldn't wait. The boat was around twenty to thirty feet in length if I recall correctly, think the boat from Jaws. We weren't dealing with some luxury cruise ship.

Out to Sea

As we begin to make the journey out to sea the waves become steep and rocky. I, being an inexperienced seaman, started to have stomach trouble. In short, I was seasick. There I was hanging over the starboard side of the boat throwing up like you wouldn't believe. I finally became accustomed to the ocean's motion and we made it out to the prime fishing spot. It took a little getting used to, but as far as you could see north, south, east, and west there was no land. We were in the middle of nowhere.

There we were, smack dab in the middle of the great Atlantic Ocean. My dad and his friend were having a grand time reeling in fish left and right. I was still struggling to get my sea legs about me. Once I caught a few fish of my own I started having fun and forgot about being so far out in the ocean. That's the thing about deep-sea fishing if you've never done it before. It's kind of a scary experience because you don't see land anywhere and your mind starts to play tricks on you.

Time passed and at a certain point we had exhausted all the fish in a certain area and so the old gnarled fisherman said he knew another spot where we could go. Everyone put away their fishing poles and settled in for a short ride to another fishing destination. That's when something really weird happened. We heard a big bang. Not like, a little noise. I mean a thud that you could not only hear, but also feel, as the boat jerked and rocked.

Time to Worry

As the old fisherman started up the engine there was a gushing sound and then the thunderous bang underneath the boat. That's when the old man said those dreaded words, "Oh no."

He was pulling up the anchor and somehow it got tangled in with the start of the motor and the anchor was yanked up fiercely into the hull of the boat. We didn't know what was going on at the time, but that was the conclusion drawn by our fearless leader. No one was diving overboard to investigate further, but the fisherman made it seem like that was the logical explanation. All I knew was all of a sudden there was water creeping up around my feet. Five minutes later there was water at my knees. The next thing I knew, all the fish that we caught were swimming freely because the water was covering everything in the boat and it was definitely starting to sink.

Now if you watched movies or television programs and you see someone grabbing the walkie-talkies screaming "Mayday, Mayday," believe me, it'll get your heart pumping fast. The fisherman was screaming "Mayday" and stating that we needed help because the boat was going down. At this point we all started scurrying towards the bow of the boat because the stern was totally submerged in salt water.

Next came the waiting as we scanned the horizon dying for a glimpse of the Coast Guard rescue boat to arrive. The Coast Guard was quite a distance away because we were out so far in deep water, but they radioed in that they were on the way.

Life jackets were tightened and I started to recall my water treading lessons from my swimming classes. In my head I pondered how I was going to tread water long enough for that Coast Guard ship to make it. I also let my mind wander about what sea creatures could be around us, hidden below the dark watery deep.

All of us were hunched up together at the bow of the boat just waiting to be rescued and this boat zooms up. The owner sees us practically bobbing there and he's saying he can't get too close because he feared he would scratch his shiny new boat.

That's something I'll never forget. There we were, practically floating in the ocean - two kids no less mind you and this guy's worried about scratching his boat. The bizarre thing was, the captain was not leaving the boat or really what was left of it. No one could convince him to get off of that boat no matter what.

It seemed like an hour long negotiation, but finally my father convinced the stranger in the other boat to let us on. He had to assure him that if the boat was scratched, he would and I quote "buy him another boat if something happened to his boat." I'm sure my father was willing to say anything just to ensure that me and the others were safe. That's something I'll always appreciate. But that man in the boat will always be a first class jerk in my book.

The Old Man and the Sea

Once we were secured on the boat my stomach was acting up again. I think my nerves were shot. I started getting seasick all over again and that man was having a fit because I might get some vomit on his boat. Let me tell you, that was an experience that I'll always remember.

A few minutes after we were rescued the Coast Guard arrived. We all watched as the old fisherman refused to be rescued by the Coast Guard, stating for the record; "the captain goes down with the ship." I thought that was just something they uttered in old movies, but that veteran sailor was living by that creed.

Within minutes his boat sunk into the Atlantic never to be pulled up again. We watched as our Captain treaded water for a few moments until the Coast Guard swooped into action and pulled him out of the water for his own safety. As we headed for shore I could see all of this taking place and still the only thing on my mind was getting back on solid land.

Looking for Land

As I gazed over the horizon I kept my eyes fixed looking for that first piece of land. It's funny how it works out. Just as soon as I saw the treelines in the distance my stomach began to ease and I felt so much better. I knew at that point we were going to be safe. We did not bring back any fish that day, but needless to say it was the most memorable fishing trip a 12-year-old could ever have had.

The thing I take away from that experience is that we all need to have hope. Hope fuels us. Hope can even keep people alive. For me on that day I think about the hope that I had to be rescued the hope that I had to make it back to land. I think about that day from time to time and I carry a bit of hope with me every day.

The Power of Hope

Sometimes your back is up against the wall and you don't know how you're going to make it and you just hope that you will. I'm no fool, yes, I know that it takes more than just hope to reach your goals. You must swing into action, but sometimes that hope is the very first step.

Before Dr. Martin Luther King put his dream into action he hoped that he would be successful. Before the first astronauts orbited the Earth they hoped they would do so safely. Before Michael Phelps set the Olympic Record for gold medals he hoped that one day he would swim in the Olympic games.

It begins with hope sometimes, so never lose track of that hope. A historical presidential campaign was run and won, based off of that one word – hope. I am not advocating any political leanings in any way, but you can see the power of simply having hope.

What are you hoping for? What do you hope to achieve? Think about those things let it fuel you let it move you forward. I *hope* that you take this information and implement it with the other chapters and develop what you need inside of you to propel you forward. I know you can achieve your goals. But you have to take these action steps. Let's dive a little deeper into hope and see how it applies in our lives as we strive to be the best we can be.

HOPE THE PRINCIPLE

"Let your hopes, not your hurts, shape your future"
- Robert H. Schuller

Perhaps you have read the story of Captain Eddie Rickenbacker and his crew when their plane fell into the Pacific. There were seven men in life rafts for twenty-one days with nothing but water and sun for as far as the eye could see.

The others in the raft didn't seem to share Eddie's state of mind. His companions clearly began to think about what lay beyond death and to think about it in terms of their own lives.

Eddie said, "at no time did I ever lose hope that we would be saved." Instead, Eddie tried to impart something to his comrades that would help them and be of great value to them. What was it? It was hope. It saved their lives.

Now, ask yourself this question. You know yourself better than anyone else, so only you can answer this. How would you have reacted to being cooped up with seven of your best friends for twenty-one days in a life raft in the middle of the Pacific?

Would you have been arguing and complaining? Would you have been the pillar of hope for your friends?

Define Hope

What is hope anyway? Hope is that amazing emotion which is unseen but, causes us to see the evidence of what we desire before we get it. It's not really faith. Faith is like the furnace in your house. Hope is like the thermostat on the wall. Hope can be regulated up and down. The more you turn it up, the more fire it creates in your belly. The more fire you create in you, the more fear you expel.

Hope is the expectation that you will get your desire, and faith is the belief that it is possible. These two are a force to be reckoned with. Together, they are more powerful than almost any other emotion inside of you. You can change the course of your destiny with hope and also with faith.

All of us react consciously to anything, which is believable, desirable and attainable in our own minds. We also react unconsciously to inner urges that cause us to get into action when suggestions are made to the subconscious.

You may react favorably, unfavorably, or neutral to some stimulus. It all depends on what the suggestions are. These suggestions have a direct impact on the hope of the individual.

You and Hope

Have you ever had to hope, against all hope, that your goal was obtainable? Have you ever, just out of sheer will and determination, forced yourself to look on the bright side of life with all the circumstances telling you you're a liar? Yes? What did you do? How did you move ahead?

Your hope is the root cause of whatever you got. Did you get your desire? You kept your hope. Did you not get what you desired? You lost your hope.

By and large, the desirable goals we obtain come when we don't lose hope. It is our hope that ensures the success.

Hope will motivate you. Hope will set a fire on the inside of you. There is nothing that you and your hope together can't accomplish. But, unfortunately, wishes are not hope. Wishes are just that, simply a daydream. Wishing is not tangible. There is no emotional attachment involved.

How can you make hope work for you? Really place your mind in a desperate frame of thought. Think back on the story of Captain Eddie. His back was against the wall. Even in my own unfortunate ocean adventure. All we had was hope at that point. Nothing else.

Hope is available. It's as close as your breath. It's in you. You have it. Just turn the thermostat up. Hope is worth its weight in gold when used. Nothing great was ever accomplished without hope.

Hope Changes Everything

Have you ever heard of Roger Bannister? On May 6, 1954 he did something that was then viewed by world experts as impossible. His success, started with hope and a vision. What did he do? He was the first person in recorded history to run and break the four-minute mile barrier.

Of course, he had to train hard for this. But it started with a hope that it could be done. Even though it had never been done before and the so-called athletic hiegharchy declared that it was unachievable. He hoped and believed it would come to fruition.

What do we learn from this? Nothing is impossible once we believe that it truly is possible. Guess what? Forty-six days later, his world record was broken. Over the next few years, that record was broken many times.

Soon, all kinds of people were breaking the four-minute barrier, from high school kids to Olympic athletes. Do you see now the power of hope and what it can do? It doesn't just change your life, but others' lives as well.

It takes time, but when you get your sub-conscious convinced that you are full of hope, watch out! You'll be filled with emotion, ready to hold on for longer than you ever thought possible. You'll be able to look into the horizon and see your goal in perfect view.

DEDICATION THE EXPERIENCE

∞

"Confidence comes from hours and days and weeks and years of constant work and dedication"

-Roger Staubach

There are very few events in life that people can call life-changing. For me personally, two of the most life-changing events was the birth of my daughter and my son.

Once you have children your life will never be the same. All you want to do is protect them and provide for them. This brings us to the subject of dedication. You may be wondering how does this relate to my children? Well it's very simple. I am dedicated to their mother and in turn to them. My dedication moves me to provide for them and to give them a comfortable life. I also strive to be a good role model for them and I am dedicated to that idea as well.

Ask yourself what are you are dedicated to or what have you dedicated your life to? Is there a cause that you are for or is there some sort of mission that you are trying to accomplish? You will never be able to fully feel satisfied in life if you are not dedicated to someone or something. As I stated for me it begins with my family and my faith.

What's Your Why?

For you it may be something completely different. But when I held my children in my arms for the first time, something happened. I knew that my life would never be the same. I knew that this little person, with those tiny eyes that were looking up to me would be depending on me. These children would be counting on me. Not just to provide school clothes or toys, but to provide them with emotional support and security. So that is why I have dedicated my work in essence to them.

Everything I do in business is a reflection of my family and my children. I want them to be proud of me. I want them to know that I am a man of integrity and I am doing things to represent the family name in a good way.

I also know that my children are watching me. They're watching my work ethic, watching what I do more than what I say. With that in mind, it makes me very cognizant of what I am doing and how I am spending my time.

I really have to attribute a lot of the credit to my wife. She was the one that told me if I was serious about going into the e-commerce apparel business, she would support me. Again, the deal was I'd have to take this very serious. She knew how I felt about my children so she tapped into that emotion and suggested that I name the company after my son.

After giving it some thought, I realized that it was a brilliant idea. She knew every time I thought about that name, I would think about my son and also my daughter. That is why I uphold the company name in such high regard making sure that each customer is satisfied.

I want to make sure that everyone is completely happy with their purchase. Why am I so passionate about that? Because I know that when people think of my company – my son's name is on the line, and I want his name to be held in high regard. That, my friend, is dedication.

Get Specific

Now let's think about this from your perspective. You'll have to identify the persons or cause that you are dedicated to. The reason for this is because it's going to drive you. If you are not dedicated to your work or to some cause, then you're really just drifting through life. If you don't have a goal or a plan of attack or in this case a dedication to something, more than likely you won't achieve much at all.

As I've stated, for me, not a day goes by where I don't think about my actions and what I'm doing and how it will effect my wife and children. I must have this dedication if I am going to move my business forward. The same is true with you. You will find this to be true - once you've made a dedication, your life is going to become much more productive.

Now it's time to ask yourself again; who or what are you dedicated to? Do you have someone or something and mind? If you don't that's fine, but let's start brainstorming on what it is that drives you. What is most important to you what people or relationships do you value? How can you use this these feelings that you have to moyou e conclusioninciple reasons ons d not if.e. They are valuable skills.If we capture the correct mindset needed, we can executve you forward in life?

There is a point in each of our lives where we all make a vow. It may be to a person, as in the case of marriage or it may be to your children. If you're not married or you don't have children that doesn't mean you can't be dedicated. I know many people who are dedicated to a cause, such as beating cancer or ending spousal abuse, or even mentoring youth. The point is, all of us have to make that dedication.

The dedication is not just to a person or a cause. In most cases it ends up being a dedication to ourselves. We can't help anyone else before we first help ourselves.

Let's now look at some principles and some points that will help you understand this concept of dedication and how it can be applied to daily life. This message is a powerful one. One that can change your life immensely. Let's dive in.

DEDICATION THE PRINCIPLE

"Most achievers I know are people who have made a strong and deep dedication to pursuing a particular goal. That dedication took a tremendous amount of effort"

- Donald Johanson

The difficult task people often face is remaining steadfast in the pursuit of their goals. Life is demanding to say the least. Stress surrounds us all on a daily basis. The capacity to manage our finances, health, relationships, career and a host of other responsibilities makes it arduous at the best of times. It's no wonder that we often feel forced to neglect those things which are important to us.

You might find your relationships fall apart when you least expect it. Your health could deteriorate or your finances could take a brutal beating. At these low moments you're perplexed at how this all came to pass without seeing the proverbial writing on the wall.

Rest assured managing life requires vigilance, dedication and commitment. After all, you're only human and from time to time things will slip right past you. The following quote serves as a reminder of the importance of the bigger picture. "Don't sweat the small stuff, because in the end its all small stuff."

The Facts

Hopefully the straightforward advice in this book will encourage you to stay dedicated to your path. Life will continuously test your resolve to see how much you desire your goal. I've seen people give up their goals after facing slight challenges. In fact, it's become fashionable - as a rite of passage for some, to trade stories on how life has dealt them a bad hand.

I often hear the reasons people recount why they gave up. It typically follows this course of dialogue; "It wasn't meant to be," or "It wasn't fun anymore," or "Life is all about having fun." The point worth mentioning is that our minds have the ability to create any mental state we impose upon it.

Through belief, you create the circumstances for giving up and thus validate it by looking for evidence to substantiate it. Think about this for a moment. How many stories or biographies about successful people have you read where the narrative involved smooth sailing or an easy path toward success? Very few I would imagine. Most success stories involve grueling challenges and a struggle to overcome the odds.

It's true, success requires discipline, hard work, perseverance, tenacity, will, courage and faith. With that in mind, here are some guidelines to staying dedicated to your goals. Life is going to throw some curveballs your way. Knowing that fact, it prepares you to face them head on.

Create Successful Habits

Many of your current day to day tasks are habitual in nature. You may have started them months or even years ago. Some of them have remained with you since childhood. The key element is to create daily habits that will draw you closer to your goal. If you're aware of negative habits, replace them with affirmative ones.

To illustrate, when I sit down to write or research I find myself wasting time surfing the internet on occasions. I know I'm buying time from the real task at hand - writing. What are some things that distract you?

In recent times, I stopped this habit by disabling my internet connection so I could focus on the task at hand. I continued this process for twelve straight days before the new habit became ingrained; thus disabling the old negative habit. I now work unaffected writing with the internet connection active, since I know I won't aimlessly waste time on social media. I have so-lidified the new habit by persisting with it.

Continue your new habit until it becomes second nature. It will take effort, but keep going until you have a firm grip on it. Phase out the old habit by replacing it with the new, empowering habit.

Be Accountable to Someone

I've always been an advocate of being accountable to someone, irrespective of how disciplined I am. Some time ago I used a number of mentors to help me stay focussed. I gained valuable insight into my work as I had the luxury of having someone else critique me, as well as make creative suggestions on areas for improvement. It's sometimes hard to accept the constructive criticism. You may find it difficult as well, but the payoff is amazing.

Being accountable may also entail making declarations of your dedication to those close to you. You might verbally or in writing, declare your intention to achieve a certain goal by a specific date. We're more likely to stay focussed on the task at hand since we don't want to disappoint others. The account-ability can help us stay the course.

Being accountable allows an impartial observer to assess your work. It is advisable to work with people who have walked your path or who have a similar experience. Alternatively, someone who is completely unrelated to your interest may also serve as a watchful eye as they offer an unbiased perspective.

Focus on Smaller Victories

Depending on the size of the goal, it's advisable to focus on smaller victories that draw you closer to your goal. For example, if your goal is to run a marathon you might allow a specified period in which to realise the goal. Take baby steps towards the finish line. Making incremental progress is wise so that you do not become overwhelmed.

In running, it might be a ten month project or more in which you undertake smaller goals along the way. Completing your first 10km run and gradually building up to competing in a longer distance event would be a logical progression.

Focussing on smaller victories along the way gives you the self confidence you need to forge ahead. Once you hit a new milestone, you become hungry for the next one. It is self empowering and a testament that you're on the right path. You might stumble upon setbacks along the way during the pursuit of smaller goals.

These are valuable lessons since they allow you to iron-out the creases so-to-speak before pursuing the larger goal. The opportunity to get it right in the build-up phase is more advantageous than getting it wrong when it matters.

Develop Hunger

Undoubtedly this remains the most challenging aspect of successful goal attainment. What makes some people pursue their goal with vehement desire while others give up when the going gets tough?

If you study human psychology and behaviour toward success, you'll notice that a large number of successful people display an insatiable hunger to succeed. Successful people are unrelenting toward the pursuit of their goal.

Sure, they experience setbacks and failures like everyone else. What sets them apart is the ability to get back on track and learn from their mistakes immediately. It's the ability to do this time and time again until they gain the prize that sets them apart.

You see, successful people believe in themselves. They've developed an inner resolve - an inner dialogue that continually feeds them with successful images, thoughts and beliefs. These inner dialogues have the power to cancel out any external misgivings that arise in the pursuit of their goal.

I invite you to find your inner conviction. Discover the reason for pursuing your goal. Why do you want it? Who will you become once you've attained it? What will life look like when you've reached your goal?

Model the people who've attained a similar goal and pursue it with passion. Successful people are adaptable. They know what they want. They're open and receptive to allowing life to show them the how in every situation.

When you develop an undying dedication to achieve a goal, roadblocks and failures are merely speed bumps instead of stop signs or red lights.

Your goal needs to be so great that it feeds and ignites your soul with purpose and meaning. You embody the goal in every cell of your being so that you become inspired to attain it. You can attain it. You will attain it.

OPTIMISM THE EXPERIENCE

❧

"Perpetual optimism is a force multiplier"
-Colin Powell

In 1996 on a Friday in June, approximately one week before high school graduation, I jumped in the car with my friends ready to play some pick-up basketball at a local park. We were laughing and joking and having a good time as usual. I was riding shotgun and enjoying the sunshine and breeze.

Even though we were cruising down the street in a totally outdated car, we didn't care, we were independent. My friend owned a Chevy Cavalier from the 1980s that really should not have been on the road. My seat belt was broken, but hey I was a teenager, thinking I was ten feet tall and bulletproof. As we approached the park we had to make a simple left turn. I could see the courts in the distance and I was ready to get a good run in.

The Turn

As my friend begin to make a left turn I could tell right away we were in trouble. He totally misjudged the timing. Barreling down on us was a pickup truck, hauling a trailer behind it. This is when things got scary. I didn't even have time to panic before I felt the full brunt of the truck smashing into my driver's door at over 50 mph. That's when the unbelievable happened.

The oversized truck smashed into us, forcing the Chevy Cavalier to flip over two or three times before it landed back on its wheels in the middle of a busy intersection. Immediately, I fled out from the car. Call it instinct. I really don't even know why, I just opened the door and ran. I didn't even stop to think if anyone else was okay. Something inside just told me I had to get out of the car and so I stumbled onto the crumbled concrete curb.

I felt blood dripping from my head and streaming down my face in steady drops. I knew I had been hurt, but I didn't know how bad. Adrenaline kicked in and kept me fully alert. As I made it to the sidewalk, passersby sprinted to me, frantically waving their arms, ushering me to the ground. I was confused and dazed, but I complied and took a seat on the grimy side-walk.

The paramedics had been called. I heard the sirens blaring. There was a fire station literally one block up the street so it didn't take long for them to arrive on the scene. As I laid, sprawled out on the concrete, I rolled my head to the side and saw my other friends stagger out of the crumpled remains of the car.

The two of them ambled towards the sidewalk and landed in a heap. One of them seemed to be uninjured, the driver, miraculously was not hurt. But the backseat passenger was severely injured. As he laid on the side of the street I could see blood gushing out from the side of his head and it looked like his ear was dangling off.

Damage Control

As we both laid there, exerting effort to make eye contact, I looked over at him thinking that he was in bad shape. He couldn't speak and all I heard was a moaning sound coming from him. I was restless, fighting and trying to get to my feet.

People were pushing me back down gently, urging me to stay still. The slickness on my face was overwhelming and I removed my shirt, and put it up to my forehead to stop the flow. I pulled the shirt away to survey the damage and found myself gasping in horror. The entire shirt was soaked with my own blood. That's when the paramedics swung into action, performing tests and stabilizing my neck.

I was transported by ambulance to a local hospital. After some time passed I was told what had transpired. I hit the car windshield and almost went through it completely. There was a huge bubbled out glass imprint in the windshield where my head had made the impact. It was a sheer miracle that I didn't fly completely through the glass, but the damage had been done.

On impact the glass shards shredded my face. My entire forehead had been sliced to bits. I even lost my right eyebrow to the damage and deep gashing. The eyebrow was completely gone. The doctor did his best to stitch my head back together, in the best way to minimize scarring, which I was grateful for. But at this point, I had still not looked into a mirror.

Take a Good Look

When I did muster up the courage to take a peek in the mirror all hope was lost for a 17-year-old teenager. This was far more horrible than unsightly acne breakouts. I was practically missing a forehead!

The doctors told me I would have to come back for special visits and have many other surgeries to correct the injuries. This nightmare was far from over. The ordeal would go on for months, as small shards of embedded glass would be forcing their way out of my head and surfacing to the skin. The skin would then have to be cut with a laser, glass removed and the skin closed back up.

Soon after all of this I realized that I could kiss the graduation ceremonies goodbye. I was in no position to walk across the stage to receive a diploma. I was in no mood for anyone to see my bandage wrapped head. I'd be wearing head wrap bandages for months and once they were removed, I had to stay out of direct sunlight.

Through the entire ordeal I had horrible headaches and was very fatigued. Depression set in rather quickly as I wondered if I would ever heal. When I asked the doctor if my eyebrow would grow back he told me the words I did not want to hear. He said he couldn't guarantee anything. I imagined going through life with only one eyebrow. I know it sounds kind of superficial, but put yourself in my shoes. At that time, as a young man, you'd think about those things and worry about it too.

Move Forward

I can still remember my first night home from the hospital. I must have slept for about twelve hours straight, but when I woke up I did something that my parents argued with me about. What did I do? When I woke up, the first thing I did was walk to the kitchen and grab my car keys.

I went directly outside and opened my car door. I was going for a drive. My mother was pleading with me not to drive considering my condition and threat of a closed head injury, but I told her that I knew I would be afraid to drive again if I didn't conquer the fear immediately.

I turned the key in the ignition and eased out the driveway. I went around the block one time to assure myself that an accident wouldn't happen every time I got in a vehicle. I made it back home within minutes and that little bit of activity just about wiped me out. I went upstairs and crawled back into bed and stared at the ceiling thinking what I would do next.

A few days later it was graduation time. Our home sat two blocks from the high school and it was rather hot that June. All the windows in the house were opened wide and I could hear the graduation ceremony taking place.

While all my friends and school colleagues were receiving applauds from their friends and family for their achievement, I just laid there in bed. My energy was still low and I felt too tired to move thinking about how I was missing out.

The only bit of good news was that my friend who was hurt in the car accident with me was recovering in a local hospital.

Our "friend," the driver of the vehicle that caused the crash – vanished. He had family in another state and because of the trouble with the accident, he immediately moved out of town and we never heard from him again.

That guy never even apologized to my face or to my friend for causing that accident. Needless to say that summer was the worst of my life, but I knew at that moment I had to make a choice. I had to make a decision.

Decision Time

I could be pessimistic or I could be optimistic. I chose to be optimistic about my future. Because of this accident and my physical limitations, I was not able to start college in the fall semester. I had to wait until the winter semester to get started, but that wasn't going to hold me back from pursuing my goals.

I was also able to obtain full-time employment during that time and as the months went by I made a full recovery. There are some people who meet me today and don't realize that I have ever been in a major accident until I mention it.

Of course along the way I had the opportunity to get plastic surgery, but I declined. I felt that I would live my life with some damage visible because it would be a reminder of what I've been through. I felt that by staying true to myself and optimistic that I would have a chance at a great future, not letting this incident define me or make me eternally negative.

We've all had horrible experiences in our lives. Maybe you were not involved in a viscous car accident but I'm sure something bad happened to you somewhere in your past. Maybe someone let you down or maybe something horrific and unexpected happened. That doesn't have to define you. That doesn't mean you have to be pessimistic about what is to come. I encourage you to stay optimistic, keep your head up and focus on all the good things that have happened.

I was able to pull myself up and stay positive. You can do the same. It doesn't matter who hurts you what happened or any bad decisions that you've made. Everything can be turned around and changed if you have optimism in your life driving and pushing you.

Let's learn a little bit more about optimism and how we can implement it into our lives. This is a very important success key for you to reach out for your dreams.

OPTIMISM THE PRINCIPLE

"One of the things I learned the hard way was that it doesn't pay to get discouraged. Keeping busy and making optimism a way of life can restore your faith in yourself"

- Lucille Ball

The power and force of optimism can never be underestimated. In fact, your personal development and growth over your lifetime depends upon it. When you are able to see the positive in every situation, you are better equipped to recognize and take advantage of opportunities that come your way.

In other words, you are more able to spring into positive action in the face of life's challenges. Plenty of research has been done that shows how optimism plays a big role in higher achievement.

Perhaps the most significant aspect of optimism is its power to transform the negative thoughts in our heads. Negative self-talk completely limits our ability to think creatively and get ourselves out of sticky situations. When we push forward in the face of negative self-talk, we are practicing optimism.

Positive self-talk greatly increases our chances of success and of moving forward in tough situations. The very fuel of success is our optimistic belief that we can impact situations and play a role in the outcome of our lives. When things begin to look dark and your mind is concocting every possible negative outcome, look for the rainbow of optimism that is always available in your mind.

Clarity

Goals give you a focus and something to look forward to. If you think about it, life would be boring without goals. Your life has a purpose, increasing your feelings of hope and optimism. Whether your goals are long term or short term, you are giving yourself a reason to get up in the morning. The link between hope and goal setting goes both ways.

Thinking about and planning your goals can increase a feeling of hope and optimism. This optimism can then boost your ability to achieve your goals. It will also assist you in planning more goals in the future.

A person with hope is able to define their goals, know how they are going to get there and are motivated to achieve them. Furthermore, hope will help a person work through any complications and so not give up when things get difficult.

It seems obvious that, if you want to have great self esteem, achieve success in life, desire increased income or want to be a leader, then what you do will directly affect this.

The Keys

There is one major key that can help you reach such goals. It's a simple but difficult goal. What could this be? Keep yourself optimistic. But what are the steps we need to practice in order to maintain our positive view of life? There are five critical keys.

Control Your Negative Thoughts of Others

This is a very easy thing to write but a very difficult habit to develop. Watch yourself carefully and note every time you think something negative about someone else. This could be your spouse, your friends or your co-workers. If you catch yourself, that's good. Eliminate the negativity. It will not help you, only hurt things.

Catch Them Being Good

This is an old phrase from behavior management. Therapists learned a long time ago that we could get children to change rapidly if we reinforced them being good. Praise works and gets results. Draw attention to the things those around you do well and watch the growth of positivity in your life.

Unexpected Giving

Giving others unexpected gifts greatly warms them up and makes them more supportive of you and of life. In fact, it can be the little things that count the most. Think about the best gift you ever received. Chances are it was not the most expensive gift. Do you see the point? A positive unexpected comment or a small token of appreciationcan go a long way in helping you and others.

Feed the Tiger

Notice what others like and appreciate, then take action. A simple example is giving a business magazine to someone who is starting their entrepreneurial journey, a donut to a donut lover, or a positive comment to someone who loves attention. Simple but doable. The gesture will be appreciated.

Look to the future

There's a lot of buzz these days around the whole concept of the Law of Attraction, which states if you feel the positive outcome you wish to achieve and believe it will come to pass, you will eventually attract that reality into your life. This is a fancy way of defining optimism.

When you are optimistic, you believe that there will be a positive outcome. When you believe that there will be a positive outcome, you are more likely to act in the positive manner that will bring about the outcome you hope for.

The future is said to be determined by whether a person strives or yields. With optimism, you always push ahead and therefore achieve what you're looking for.

There was an interesting study done by Robert Shuman in 1979 that speaks about the loss of optimism. When Shuman was practicing psychology at a children's hospital, he suffered from great mental torment and was hospitalized for back pain. He was later diagnosed with debilitating multiple sclerosis. He fell into a state of great helplessness, anguish, and torment, and decided to document these feelings that he knew so many others in similar chronic situations were plagued with.

His notes culminated in his book *The Psychology of Chronic Illness*. Shuman's book was significant because it brought to our understanding how chronic illness with no cure ruins optimism in individuals-perhaps for the rest of their lives. Once power over our own lives is lost, our optimism is lost as well.

The power of optimism is the power to successfully navigate and overcome life's greatest challenges. Optimism can be learned. You need not be a born optimist to experience the benefits of optimism. In reality, optimism is a choice that we can all make.

We all have the power to observe our negative thoughts and compulsive actions. We have the power to be aware of ourselves and our past that influences our current actions. When we are finally able to clearly see what we are doing and understand what we are thinking, we then have the power to choose optimism.

DETERMINATION THE EXPERIENCE

❦

"Failure will never overtake me if my determination to succeed is strong enough"

\- Og Mandino

In 2001 I was your typical college student, stressed and overworked. I was also engaged to be married. The problem is I also worked full-time. No, not 32 hours a week. I held down a blue collar job, pulling in 40-50 hours a week. I'm talking dirty blue jeans and finger nails, chemicals and fumes with your traditional level of dirty grime tossed in for good measure.

In a few months I would have a new wife and apartment plus a lot more responsibility than I even realized and I was running out of time. Running out of time? Yes, I'd wanted nothing more than to finish up my Bachelors degree in Business Administration. Yes, the degree that all my co-workers tell me will be worthless.

Have you ever watched Good Will Hunting? Yea, that pretty much sums up my circle of employees, minus the Boston accent and unfortunately I don't have Matt Damon character's genius IQ. Despite the naysayers I felt the degree couldn't hurt my resume.

I'm no educational elitist or even preach that people need to attend higher education. Some of the wisest men and women I've ever come across never stepped foot on a University campus.

Back to my situation. I was getting close to running over the four years I'd allotted myself to graduate on time. I could've went slower, stretched it out, took my time and "found myself." That just wasn't me though. I didn't have the traditional college experience per se, so I just wanted closure.

At a crossroads I had a decision to make. It's either have all these responsibilities, being newly married, working full-time in the grease pit *and* be a full-time student or dual enroll at two institutions in my last semester.

The Choice

I decided to dual enroll and "go for it." What does going for it look like? Well I'll tell you. I needed 32 credits to complete my Bachelors degree. That's like taking two semesters and cramming it into one. The local community college had courses I could take that will go towards my degree. If I signed up for those, as well as the courses at the college that I attended, I would be able to finish my degree on time. Just in time for the wedding.

Well, actually I would be finishing up that last semester during our first few months of marriage. Still, I feel like it would be better to just get that course work out-of-the-way rather than to prolong things any further. I also definitely did not want to take summer classes.

I've never been the strongest student, but my determination has always gotten me through to make sure that I have succeeded in my classwork so I figured this shouldn't be any different. I decided to dive in and go for it.

I waltzed into the administration buildings at both institutions and dual enrolled, making sure I have the 32 credits needed to complete the degree. I knew this will be a challenge but it's a challenge that I was up to tackle and there's only one way to find out if you can do something and that is to do it.

Busy Busy Busy

Needless to say for the next few months I was busier than I had ever been before. Did I think I could get a 4.0 on all the courses? Of course not and if I'm being honest I wasn't headed towards valedictorian anyway. All I know is that I want to complete the task.

Let me tell you, my decision to attempt this wasn't a popular one with friends and family. I heard a lot of the naysayers use words like crazy and foolish. That just fueled me even more because I knew it had to be done. Sometimes you reach a point where you just know you have to get over the hump you have to achieve a certain goal.

Have you ever wanted to achieve something even though you know it would be hard? That's the position I found myself in. Now please bear in mind I had been in school for the past four years and all the while working full-time 40+ hours a week so I was tired, really tired.

I didn't even mention the roughly 30-minute drive each way to campus. Three nights a week, class didn't get out until 10 pm. Tack on that thirty-minute ride home and that doesn't leave much time for a social life. Now you're possibly seeing why I was in such a hurry to get the coursework behind me. Even though I was close to the finish line I felt like I couldn't let things drag out another minute.

My plan of attack was to be determined and disciplined. I would have to schedule my time wisely. That would be little time for fun. But that's what life is about. Sometimes you have to sacrifice the fun and put in the work. You just keep telling yourself it'll pay off in the end.

Counselors from both school advised against "my plan" and we're not very happy or supportive. Why? For one, it was more work than any student especially one working full-time could really handle and the odds of success were stacked against me.

They doubted success with my track record and here is where I'll remind you that I wasn't the strongest student. My transcript may or may not impress you, depending on your point of view. But what I told the counselors is the plain and un-cut truth. I wasn't interested in being an honor student. I was interested in completing my goal and that's what I set out to do.

Once the semester got rolling boy did things get very diffi-cult. I was up to my eyeballs in writing papers and doing course-work. My friends probably thought I had forgotten about them and my fiancé maybe was wondering the same thing. I juggled it all the best I could. As it came down to the wire I was up against it, I had so many papers that needed to be written. But I buckled down and found a way to get it done.

Waiting Game

As I waited for the results of each class I was very tense as you could imagine. Sure, if I failed one or two of the courses I could elect to take them over again in the summer session and probably still be done in time for Fall. That would be a last resort. I had really set this up as a challenge between myself. At some point in the semester, I myself wanted to if I could complete the coursework. I almost made it a personal challenge.

How far could I push myself? How much could I take? Would I be successful? The question lies out there for each one of us to answer. What is it that you want to achieve? What goals do you have? What are the challenges you face? How can you be successful? The answer is, it will take determination grit and will. As they always say, it takes blood sweat and tears, but the thing is you can do it.

Now, you're probably wondering how did I fare on my quest to complete 32 credit hours of college coursework in one semester while working full-time and planning a wedding? Well, I'll first admit that I didn't have to do much of the wedding planning. In reality, it was more like just show up for the wedding ceremony and I'm grateful for that. The coursework and the mental preparation to complete the papers and the testing, yea, that was on my shoulders. Squarely on my shoulders.

Guess what? I was able to complete all the coursework with

passing grades, emphasis on passing grades, not stellar grades. I fondly look back on this time period as one of my greatest accomplishments. Why?

I have to admit that it was very challenging for me. Perhaps you are a great student and you thrive in the traditional learning environment. If that is the case, then this would not have been so challenging for you.

But myself, I struggle to stay alert as soon as a lecture begins. I was the sleeping kid in the back of your high school classroom. Even today I struggle when a meeting or lecture goes longer than say ten minutes. I seriously didn't know if I was going to make it. But I did make it, never mind that it was barely and by the skin of my teeth. The point is, I made it through.

Aftermath

So here I am today, many years later, telling you that no matter what you're facing, you can make it through. All of us have something inside of us that is more amazing than we realize. The sad thing is that we underestimate ourselves and sell ourselves short.

Right now, I want you to tell yourself you're not going to doubt yourself anymore. Whatever goal you have, whatever dreams you're trying to achieve, you can reach for them if you set goals and you are determined.

I heard a quote once that says if you know your why for doing something then how you'll get it done will not matter. It will be of so much importance that you'll just make a way. Enough about me and this trip down memory lane.

Let's dig into some principles and some practical advice that will help you to understand determination on a deeper level. You will also see how you can train yourself to achieve a high level of determination and apply it to your life as a gentleman.

DETERMINATION THE PRINCIPLE

❦

"I've known entrepreneurs who were not great salespeople, or didn't know how to code, or were not particularly charismatic leaders. But I don't know of any entrepreneurs who have achieved any level of success without persistence and determination"

- Harvey Mackay

At the end of the day, the most successful individuals are those that keep trying, even when it seems like there is nothing left to fight for. The ability to persist longer than anyone else is the one quality that will guarantee great success in life. That endurance is vital for your success. If you keep working hard every day and stay persistent, you will blossom. Here are a few more tips to help you stay determined and reach your goals.

Start each day by visualizing your goals. Remember you are the director of your life's movie and your imagination is your preview for everything you will achieve. Try to "see" your goals as if they already exist. Doing so will activate all of your available mental powers and help you attain your goals. If you are new to this, you may be a bit uncomfortable with this - it works!

Do not be afraid to unlock your potential. You have the ability to achieve anything you put your mind to. Just look at everything you have achieved so far. That was just the preparation for everything you will accomplish in the future. Decide to be uncomfortable with the status quo and to really go after what you want in your life.

Grab the Bull by the Horns

Take charge. It is you who is responsible for whatever you achieve today, tomorrow and months down the road. You are responsible for everything you think, say and do and for everything you will become in the future. You must stop making excuses and blaming others for your failures. Instead, know it is up to you and work on your goals each and every day. A mentor taught me years ago to not get caught up in our "stories." What are you telling yourself about your abilities and about how successful you can be?

Create your future. Refuse to accept that there are limitations on what you can do, be or have in the months and years ahead. Continually think about and plan your future. You will find the resources to create any life that you desire. It is amazing what will appear if you stay committed and on course. I know now that what I think about I attract. What is I ask for usually shows up in one way or another, sooner or later. And what I can measure and track, I can change.

Clarify your values. If you are going to set goals you need to think about what is the most important to you. It is your innermost values that define you as a person. Do not change or stray away from what you feel is right for you.

Think about your beliefs. Those beliefs include what you think about your own abilities and about the world around you. What you believe you can achieve. Knowing this in your heart will have more of an impact on your feelings and actions than any other factor. Know that you can be successful. Just know it. Go to work and do the work.

Be Exact

Next, define your true goals. This will help you stay persistent. It is up to you to decide what you want to accomplish with your life. Clarity is essential for happiness and living up to your true potential. With that you can find a central purpose to build your life around.

Try to find one single goal that will help you achieve all of your other goals. I am a huge believer in setting goals and writing them down. Review them at least quarterly. Don't worry if they are a moving target meaning you don't achieve all your goals in the time frame you thought you would. That is normal.

Do not be afraid to start from the beginning. Determine you exact situation and be both honest and realistic when you are thinking about what you want to accomplish in the future. I have heard that most of us over estimate what we can get done in a year but very much underestimate what we can get done in five years.

Think bigger picture and longer term. One of the biggest mistakes people make is not giving their business enough time in terms of the time spent each week and the time spent working it before they give in or up.

Unlock your creativity. Everyone has the ability to be creative and solve problems. If you are not meeting your goal, do not be afraid to come up with a new and better way than what you are currently doing.

Anyone can tap into their intelligence to overcome any obstacle and achieve their goals. People do so all the time. Everyone has their moments where they feel like they are beating their head against the wall, but that is just part of the journey to success.

Eliminate all obstacles. Your success boils down to your ability to solve problems and remove obstacles that stand in the way of your goal. Although you may make mistakes at times, if you just keep trying you will achieve your goals. Don't let the naysayers get to you. Don't let something that isn't that important to you stand in the way of something that is very important to you!

Your Circle

Be sure to associate with the right people. The choices you make in regards to the people whom you live, work and socialize with will affect your success. You should only associate with people that you actually like, respect and admire. If you want to be a successful and good person, you should only associate with others who strive to be the best.

We are the sum total of the five people we spend the most time with. Who are the five people you spend the most time with? Are they pulling you up and lifting you up or dragging you down?

Do not procrastinate, stay persistent. Learn how to manage your time well and to double and triple your productivity. To do this learn and practice proven time management principles. I love the book *The One Minute Manager* by Ken Blanchard. In the book he teaches to not get distracted by trivial matters and always set priorities before you begin.

At the end of each day, take a moment to review and reevaluate your goals and objectives. Make sure you are on track and that you are still working on the things that are most important to you. Be ready to adapt your plan, as it is needed.

Celebrate at the end of the day by focusing on what you did get done and what you moved forward. Don't look at the never ending to do list and feel frustrated for what you didn't get done. I have a process where at the beginning of the week I write out the top five things to get done that week.

I will get a lot of other things done too but if by Thursday, I haven't gotten the top five things done then I focus much more on those. It is so easy to be busy and to get distracted and not get to the most important things.

Remain flexible and roll with the punches. Keep your goals in mind, but do not be afraid to try an alternative way of meeting them. Who knows, there may be a solution that is newer, better, faster and cheaper. If something is not working, be willing to try a different approach.

Being consistent and persistent with your goals and your daily activities is going to get you where you want to go.

DRIVE THE EXPERIENCE

❦

"I do it because I'm driven to do it"
- Bob Dylan

For the past few years I've been a huge fan of podcasts. I listen to them in a wide range of subjects. Some of them I listen to for entertainment some of them for information. I appreciate the vast variety of personalities that I get to hear. I love the informative content and I am also a fan of learning. There's nothing better for me than when I can pop in my headphones, learn something new, and have a laugh or two while expanding my mental horizons.

I know podcasting is getting more and more popular everyday. That got me to thinking. I thought to myself, that maybe I could give it a shot. Maybe I could get behind the microphone and talk to people. I wanted interview other business owners, stylists, people in the fashion industry, authors and business coaches. I thought it could be great for networking. But how would I get started?

I knew nothing about podcasting, only how to play one on my iPhone. At that point I did what I always do when I have a bright idea. I ran the thought past my wife and she told me what she always tells me.

"You better do your research," she said. So I did. The thing is sometimes even when you do your research, you realize maybe there are some aspects of something that are a bit over your head. My shortcoming was the technical aspect of it all. I didn't let that stop me though. What I did was tap into the resources that I had around me. What did that look like?

Research

I started asking friends and colleagues if they knew anyone that could help me get this thing off the ground. I went on YouTube look up tutorials and found lots of good information there. Then I went to Google and started reading every article I could about putting a podcast together. Next, I signed up for a course to learn about how to produce podcast the equipment that would be needed the investment and things like this.

Still, I knew my technical skills may not be enough to get the job done so I recruited others to help edit and produce the podcast. I reached out to friends to see if they wanted to get involved. I reached out to professional colleagues and contacts to ask them if they be willing to come on to be interviewed as a featured guest.

Guess what? Most of them said yes. Before I know it I had assembled a small team ready to tackle the task of producing our first podcast and with our limited knowledge we begin to get started.

My favorite motivational speaker in the world, Les Brown, says to leap and grow your wings on the way down. In other words, start before you're ready. Les always says, 'you don't have to be great to get started but you've got to get started if you're going to be great.' That is a phrase I like to live by.

Diving In

We dived in and in under a month our first podcast was live on iTunes. Was it the greatest bit of audio that you'll ever hear? I highly doubt it. Sad to say, I'm a little embarrassed at our pilot episode. But guess what? We didn't stop there. We kept going, kept improving and soon things got better. The sound quality is getting better, the content is improving and even my interviewing skills are improving each week.

The point I want you to take away from this is that there were many obstacles on the road to establishing a podcast. As I stated, I really knew nothing about podcasting besides the fact that I enjoyed them. But that wasn't going to stop me. Within a few months the show racked up over fifty great reviews and The Life of a Gentleman Podcast is really picking up steam.

You have to ask yourself important questions from time to time. What is something that you want to do? What are you afraid to do? What is it that you think you cannot do? We all have things that we want to achieve but we're nervous about going for it.

You have to ignore the doubts, shove them to the side and rush into the task that you want to tackle. Believe me, once you are in the middle of that fight you were going to find a way to make it happen and come out with a positive result.

You can procrastinate or wait around thinking about things, but it will get you nowhere. I call this paralysis by analysis. You can literally spend so much time planning and not implementing action that it becomes detrimental to you.

Go for It

I had a supervisor at one time in my employment that would tell me, "just make it happen." I would ask him what he wanted to have accomplished and sought some guidance. He would quickly dismiss me from his office and remind me to just make it happen. Before long, I started to make things happen. I started diving into tasks and going for it. I learned that it was better to beg for forgiveness rather than to ask for permission.

I started to gain more confidence with each win and I carried this mentality over into the podcast endeavor. At the beginning I was nervous, wondering, how we would pull it altogether. Where would I get the art for a podcast? What type of microphones would we need? How would we get the distribution? All good questions but it really doesn't matter. Why? Because you're never going to find out if you don't get in the game.

Drive is going to push you. Drive is going to motivate you. Drive is going to make sure that you keep striving with every fiber of your being. Deep down in your gut you may have some doubt. Silence that doubt. You will make it, but you have to possess grit and determination. Let's examine deeper about what drive is and how we can use it to our advantage.

DRIVE THE PRINCIPLE

"If you don't drive your business, you will be driven out of business"
- B. C. Forbes

D rive is one of the most important success factors. To have desire is one thing, but to have drive is another thing entirely. All success stories begin with a drive. The extent to which you succeed in any endeavour is largely influenced by certain success factors, and in this case - the intensity of your drive. Your drive for what you want to achieve must be so strong that you would find it hard to sleep at night.

You literally can lose sleep over thinking about your future plans. It becomes such an obsession that it dominates your thinking, making it difficult to concentrate on anything else. If you can't get that wound up about something, it's only an idea or a passing thought, not really a drive.

Intensity

A drive is intense and urgent as opposed to something that is nice to have, like desiring an ice cream. It is to success what rocket propellant is to a rocket engine. It is a burning desire that propels a person into action. A burning desire is creative power that has to manifest or express itself in the external world. It is an emotional force that attracts.

The emotion attached to your drive moves you towards your desired outcome and magnetically draws your desired outcome towards you. A drive has a sense of desperation to it and, as an ingredient of success, it is comparable to air, the most basic element for life's sustenance. Can you survice without air? Can your dreams survive without drive? The answer to both questions is no.

Success is something that we are all capable of achieving. We can all be successful in every area of our lives as long as you follow the universal rules that are already laid out. You'll find success after forming certain habits and consistently applying them in every area of your life.

With persistence and patience anyone can be the person they always dreamed of becoming. Those habits you need to develop will teach you to think, talk, and act in a certain way. Here's a fun little tip, if you apply these five principles in one area of your life, you'll be able to watch your own success in that one area while watching the others fail.

Understand Your Vision

Have a clear picture as to what you want to achieve and become. Keep that picture at the forefront of your mind each and every day. If you do that perfectly everything you do will be driven towards a single goal and it will motivate you to take the correct path. Start with the end in mind and you won't need anyone else to do it for you.

Believe in Yourself

Know without a doubt that you can do it. Believe that success is your only option. You cannot afford to even consider failing. No matter what, you need to know that there is something deep inside pushing you to your goals, through the good times and the bad. Protect yourself from the negativity in the world, it's not going to do you any good. Surround yourself with successful people and successful thoughts. Successful does not mean rich or wealthy. Let's make that very clear.

It's a fact that you will mirror the five people who you spend the most time with. We have all heard that birds of a feather flock together. Look around and you'll see a whole bunch of pigeons, but you rarely see an eagle. What do you want to be? A pigeon or an eagle? If your circle of friends are not successful people, then be the bigger person and help them become successful people with you. Help others to soar like an eagle and break away from the common crowd.

Live Your Life with Passion

Have you ever wondered why some people wake up every morning to do the same thing day in and day out. They are miserable, but they never change. What kind of life is that? Wouldn't it make more sense to do something that would make you absolutely energized?

The goal is to get paid for doing something that you would be willing to do for free. Follow your passion and the income will come to you. If it's not income you seek, then peace of mind will still come your way.

No two people follow the same path, we've all got different things in our life that we love and the key to understanding is to find out what your truly passionate about and live your life according to that passion. There's nothing wrong with Mondays. There is only something wrong with the choices we make on Mondays.

Make Positive Affirmations

Habitually tell yourself out loud what you will achieve and commit to that affirmation by taking action consistently. Decide to take whatever steps you feel are necessary to help you achieve your goals and honor that commitment by following through.

Don't let other people tell you how to achieve their goals, they don't have a firm grasp on your reality. There will be naysayers. Ignore them. A lot of people think it might sound crazy to talk to themselves, to get over that make those affirmations to someone close to you and ask them to hold you to that commitment.

Make A Plan and Stick To It

You can pretend to make commitments every single day. The fact of the matter is, saying something doesn't make it true.

A positive attitude won't change the world. Taking action will change the world. Having a plan on paper will give you something to look at, will give you a template to work from.

We are so much more likely to have success when we write down our goals on paper and look at them everyday. We can visualize these goals and then they will become real to us. Remind yourself every time you look at it that each time you take a step in that direction you're one step closer to achieving your goals. Be consistent. No days off, pays off.

Give More Than You Receive

When trying to progress remember one thing, the world does not revolve around you. Always think in terms of the other person. Follow the Golden Rule, do unto others as you would want done unto yourself. Be generous to everyone you come in contact with, you never know who's watching.

Be patient. Success doesn't come overnight. Success is an attitude and a thought process that one learns over the course of their life. Each one of us is the only one who can determine whether or not they are successful, you don't need to worry about other peoples opinions. Opinions are like bellybuttons, everybody has one. My vision for you, may be different than your vision for yourself and vice versa.

Make a plan and follow through. If you feel successful, then you are successful. Success is a mindset. There is no tangible way to measure it. It cannot be determined based on money or status. It is only determined by the way you feel when you look in the mirror.

ADAPTABILITY THE EXPERIENCE

$$\backsim\!\!\infty\!\!\frown$$

"It is not the strongest or the most intelligent who will survive but those who can best manage change"

— Leon C. Megginson

In 2014, I started looking at some fashion blogs and noticed the trendy fashion accessory, lapel pins. I thought those fabric boutonnieres looked pretty dapper. I always try to look for something unique that I can add to my wardrobe that will help me stand out from the crowd or show off a little bit extra personality but in a classy subdued way and I thought these lapel pins would be just the thing.

Not many people if anyone in my area where wearing them so I wanted to have one to set myself apart from the crowd. But then I noticed the price point for them and it gave me pause. At that time, what I found is they were around $35 for one lapel pin. One thing I'll admit is that I don't like to overpay for items. Some people will call it being cheap, but I call it being frugal. What did I do?

I had it in my mind that I could probably make a lapel pin. It didn't look like it was that hard. I figured, a few pieces of fabric and a pin - fasten it on, bingo. It couldn't be that hard. Boy was

I wrong. It took me quite some time and a lot of trial and error, but eventually I made a lapel pin that I thought was suitable.

Show Time

I planned to wear my homemade lapel pin to an upcoming upscale event. When I walked into the venue everyone was looking at me with interest and noticing the lapel pin. I was pleased to receive several compliments. Things were going well.

There's always that one nosy person who goes a little too far. In this case it was someone I knew well. They decided to dig a little bit deeper. They came closer, reached out and touched my DIY project. They pulled it up a bit and noticed the many design flaws, including globs of glue on the backside.

They told me I had it all wrong and truthfully they were right. The way that I had designed it and put it together was not perfect. I knew that, but I just wanted to get the initial prototype rolling.

After several design attempts, in just a few weeks later I was able to master the design. I purchased the necessary materials and started to mass produce my first batch of lapel pins. With the help of a few friends we had them assembled. A small business was born.

Start Small

At this point you have to remember I was starting off with literally a couple hundred dollars invested into the business. I tend to be very cautious and don't like to spend a lot of money, time or resources on things when I'm not sure of the outcome. But at the same time when I see a good thing I go for it.

Before you know it we were selling so many lapel pins you would not believe it. At one point we had over 200 unique styles available for sale on the website. But then the lapel pin craze caught on and before you know it there was lapel pin companies popping up everywhere on the Internet and advertising on social media. At that point I knew when others zig I would have to zag. That means you have to be adaptable.

Roll with the Punches

You cannot be afraid to change and grow your business in different directions. This can even apply in your personal life and not just in business. Perhaps my experience will give you a few ideas.

When I found the market for lapel pins getting too saturated I started to expand the business into other accessories such as neckties, pocket squares, cufflinks and the like. And before you know it, the website had many more options for gentlemen.

As time moved on I started to find that there was even more competition on the horizon. Other entrepreneurs started diving into men's accessories and the field was becoming quite crowded. That'you e conclusioninciple reasons ons d not if.e. They are valuable skills.If we capture the correct mindset needed, we can executs That is why you have to be adaptable. This is a valuable skill. If we have the correct mindset needed we can execute change? What did I decide to do? I decided to launch a monthly subscription club.

As you can see, the business kept changing. I had to keep expanding and morphing it into something different in order to keep things going in the right direction. I decided to offer one necktie plus four accessories for a $25 per month subscription and that way everyone could get value and also a unique coordinated look the easy way.

A few months into getting this subscription service off the ground I included a bow tie with the package and boy did I experience some backlash. There were men who emailed in, saying they didn't know how to tie a bow tie. Other guys just weren't bow tie people. So then, I had to adapt once more.

I produced a bow tie club, specifically designed for people who love bow ties. The bow tie lovers could get what they wanted and the necktie people would also be happy. Two bowties for $16 per month is the deal that no bowtie fan can ignore.

Keep Moving

You know the funny thing about this whole business experience is that I never knew how to execute the next step. I'd never started a subscription service company. I never knew anything about how to start an e-commerce company to sell anything online. Did that stop me? No!

I did my research. I was able to get it started. I got the ball rolling and then as the ball started rolling off course, I adjusted. There are always going to be pitfalls and obstacles that you'll have to move around. Sometimes you can dive over them. Other times you'll have to dig under them or bust right through them.

The point I'm trying to stress is that my business has grown exponentially and it has evolved in so many ways. I'm glad that it has because it's afforded me the opportunity to learn new things, unique ways of doing commerce and creative marketing.

Imagine where I'd be if I would've just stuck with only selling lapel pins? Where would I be? How much revenue with the company make? Not much. According to Forbes magazine 8 out of 10 businesses fail within the first 18 months. By being adaptable and having adaptability as part of the business model, I was able to survive.

Change is Good

By changing, innovating with the times and the market we survived. Are you locked into doing everything one certain way? Do you do things a certain way because that's the way it has always been done? It's time to start thinking outside the box. It's time to start implementing adaptability into your business or personal life. By being adaptable you're going to open up so many more doors of opportunity for yourself. It's time to step out of your comfort zone.

Life begins at the end of your comfort zone. What does that mean? It means you need to try new things. Don't get stuck in a rut. Don't forget to be creative. Don't be afraid to try new things.

Let's look at some principles that are going to help you with adaptability and implementing this important aspect into your everyday life.

ADAPTABILITY THE PRINCIPLE

"There can be no life without change, and to be afraid of what is different or unfamiliar is to be afraid of life."

— Theodore Roosevelt

Adapting can mean two things, either its adapting to good things or bad things. So if you adapt yourself to bad things, it will bring bad consequences to you. If you adapt to good or positive things it will reward you by giving you what you have worked towards achieving.

Now I know that every one has their good and bad habits. The key point here is to commit to yourself that your going to step away from your bad habits and start with new and good habits, habits that will improve your current situation.

Here's an example that I hope makes sense to you. If you know you have a lot of debt but you still go shopping and spend a lot of money, you know for a fact that what you are doing something wrong there. By making a budget for your shopping or just doing it only when you really need it you will save money. This takes self control. Having that extra money to payout your debt is something that I know will be a relief for you. You simply have to prioritize.

Something New

It is also important that you develop new skills because it enables you to adapt to change. You also have to work on your new skills by being abreast with new technology in your chosen profession. Some people find it difficult getting a job simply because they are not compliant with the new technology of that profession.

There can be few professionals who have been unaffected by the rapid pace of change which has influenced the professions over the past decade. Professionalism relies increasingly on an ability to respond quickly to changing market conditions, to client requirements and to the influences of government policies.

We are all being encouraged to embrace change and foster innovation. To adapt to these changes we need new skills. No longer can keeping up to date be optional. It is increasingly central to professional and organizational success.

Success Story

I tend to translate lessons of success from those in the athletic field. Duke University Coach Mike Krzyzewski became the winningest coach in men's college basketball. I will confess, I am not a Duke fan. But as a sports fan, I have to marvel at the efficiency of that basketball program. Somehow they find a way to compete at the highest level every year. Coach Krzyzewski's adaptability in changing as the game of basketball has changed is a testament to his greatness.

Can you adapt? When things change, you have to change. To adapt is not giving up on who you are, it is you evolving. Your principles don't change but how you achieve your goals do. Understand that the one who is steadfast on doing things the way they have always done them will not survive. I use the word survive but this is not about survival, it's about your evolution. It's about recognizing when you have to change. Adapting will always equate to longevity.

Adaptability Wins

In everything that we do, change will always be a factor. In the business world, concepts on doing business change. Technology is always changing. In order to remain competitive, you have to adapt. In order to remain relevant, you have to adapt. You have to be a flexible person. To remain rigid when the circumstance calls for being flexible will be a detriment to your success.

Never feel that you cannot make new plans. Plans are necessary. On the contrary, having the foresight to expect changes will aid in your response time to react.

I have often wondered why change is so hard. I understand that people resist change because of the unknowing. The thought of embarking on a path that has not been traveled by you can be frightening yet you know where you want to end the destination.

You know where you want to go. They say insanity is repeating the same thing over and over but expecting different results. We call it insanity, but is that the result of fear?

No Fear

The fear to change, is why people refuse to adapt to situations. If you want to be successful, you have to get out of your comfort zone. You have to change. You have to be able to adapt. If you want to achieve a goal, you have to change. If you want to fulfill a dream, you have to change. It starts with changing the way you think. You have to believe that you can do it!

When we resist change, we are unsure of ourselves. We don't always have the faith in ourselves like we should. A measure of confidence is needed. Being able to adapt shows just how much faith you have in yourself. In order to overcome failures, you have to be able to change. Change is making adjustments. Change is a part of progression. Change is a way of life.

In a world that changes constantly, adapting will guide your imagination. It will open you up to new possibilities. A different way of thinking does not disrupt on what you want your outcome to be. It only changes how you get there. The most important object is to reach your goal.

Great leaders understand that they must be willing and able to adapt to changing finances, varying needs, adapting to a change in terms of missions and goals. Leaders should also remain open to alternatives and varying strategies.

In other words, those wanting to lead, must become quick on their feet. You have to change quickly. You can't drag your feet. Trust your gut and make the changes where needed.

Plan Ahead

How can someone be adaptable while maintaining thir principles, goals and objectives? Most of us become personally involved and entwined in our initial approach, better known as our Plan A. We become somewhat unwilling to adapt in any manner, often becoming somewhat intransigent in terms of our approaches. The reality is that one must pay attention to financial changes and the needs or desires of his organization.

There is rarely any one way that is the absolute manner to get something done or achieved. The approach should be adaptable, as long as one maintains his focus on the true goals and needs. Don't fall into the trap of having tunnel vision. Be open to changes. Why are so few in positions of leadership unwilling to commit to the strategic planning process?

When one truly strategically plans, he analyzes all relevant factors in an organized, indepth manner, in order to discover the best and most effective way to proceed and to understand alternatives.

If Plan A stumbles, be ready immediately and seamlessly to adapt with a Plan B, C, and so on. Thinkin with strategy will be benefit to you. Be more than willing to change, when necessary. It will be necessary.

RESOURCEFULNESS THE EXPERIENCE

$$\infty$$

"The measure of a person's strength is not his muscular power or strength, but it is his flexibility and adaptability"

— Debasish Mridha

In 2008 the economic recession was in full swing. The dot com boom has busted. I was living in the heart of the Midwest and GM, Ford and Chrysler were laying people off like crazy. The auto industry was the heartbeat of our state and it was having the life sucked right out of it. Each day there was stories on the news showing us how people by the thousands were fleeing out of the state as if there was a nuclear bomb headed towards us. The economy was truly in the toilet.

I'd been working on my job for a few years and was promoted to an entry level management position. I'd been married for a while now and had a two-year-old child at home to care for. I had a lot of responsibility on my plate and I was also just getting started with my writing career. But that's when the bad news hit. You know it's bad news when two of the upper management come your way and ask if they can speak with you privately. That's what you call a dead giveaway.

As we walked to the office I prepared my mind for the worst. When we got there, they set me down and explained that the position I held needed to be eliminated in order to help the company financially. In short we were downsizing and I was out. I was thinking I would be gone that day or the end of the week but they assured me I was going to be "phased out." I asked what that meant and discovered that I had about three months before the position would come to an end.

Stay or Go?

As I went home that afternoon I thought about things. Should I stick it out until the end? Should I immediately start looking for other employment? After much thought I decided to make it my new full-time job, to look for a new full-time job. Yes, I'd go to work every day, clock in and out and do my job, but my real focus would be finding new gainful employment.

Many people are put in this position everyday and some decide to wait it out to the end. I wanted to do the exact opposite. I wanted to be proactive. I started talking to people, asking around, if they knew of any open positions.

Meanwhile, back at the office, word had spread like wildfire that I was going to be let go. That's really an uncomfortable situation, especially when you're one of the only people that is being effected by the downsizing. All of the other employees were safe. Some of them would come in with their well wishes and sad faces, telling me they hoped for the best.

Like I said in our community, the economy was extremely tight and there weren't many jobs available. It was nothing unusual to personally know a handful of people that were unemployed and miserable. I was determined not to join that group. I was very very deliberate in my efforts to find new employment.

After much persistence I was able to get an interview with a mid sized manufacturing company. I knew that this would be my chance to get my foot in the door. I wasn't satisfied with just placing my foot in the door. I was planning to knock that door completely off the hinges.

Be Prepared

My plan was to wow the interviewers. I was going to make it so they could not tell me no. The funny thing was that this was a new field for me. I'd worked in production, so I knew deadlines, but this was product manufacturing. I was determined to sell myself and to find a way to show that I could handle the position.

In order to prepare for the opportunity at hand I decided to go on YouTube. You're probably wondering what does YouTube have to do with the opportunity for a new job? Well, I'll tell you. There were so many tutorials that I found online. There were sample interviews, outlining what to say or what not to do. I loved the job interview scenarios where people acted out different scenarios and I placed myself in those different positions.

I also was prepared for any question that they would throw my way. In addition, I also had questions prepared to present to them. In short, when I walked into that interview I was owning that space.

All the hard work paid off and I actually landed the management position and before long I was doing extremely well on the new job. In fact, in under six months I received a promotion and another one soon after that. Why was that the case? I continued to do research and study each night, learning more about that industry and how I could bring my unique skills to the table to make myself a more valuable employee.

Satisfaction

I would often laugh to myself, as I recalled when I told my old job that I was leaving. They were absolutely shocked. They thought for sure they would have me for the duration of time that they needed to phase out my position. Instead of them sending me off with a cardboard box, I left on my own terms.

There was no waiting around and hoping for them to maybe change their mind. I was going to move on and do so with a positive attitude. You're probably facing some sort of obstacle right now. You're probably wondering how you're going to deal with this situation. I'm encouraging you to deal with it headon. Do your research and figure out different ways to look at things. There has to be some kind of other angle to make it around or over your roadblock.

So many people are so quick to lay down and die. Many choose to just deal with the situation they are given or the hand that they are dealt. But you don't have to live this way. You can be proactive. You can be resourceful. That is the way that you can have a positive outcome, inside of a negative situation.

Remember that a setback is just a set up for a comeback. You may be down, but you're not out. I need you to pick up the pieces right now and start reassembling them in a different way so that you can have success.

Let's look deeper at resourcefulness and see how you can implement this into your life so that you can achieve whatever you have in your mind fixed on.

RESOURCEFULNESS THE PRINCIPLE

 ∾

"Life's too short to hang out with people who aren't resourceful"
- Jeff Bezos

E ver felt like no matter how hard you try you still can't focus on completing the task at hand? Whatever the task, however important it is, you just can't seem to be able to concentrate on it for longer than thirty seconds. We have all been there before.

It's a problem often referred to as procrastination, and it's something all of us experience. But at times where a deadline is approaching, we freeze. Even worse, we never get started. That is commonly referred to as paralysis by analysis. You have to get yourself into gear.

The law of inertia tells us that a body in motion stays in motion. The same thing goes for projects, creative ideas, daily tasks, half-written emails, and that thing you stopped working on to read this book. Hopefully this book can serve as the kick in the pants that you need. When you interrupt a task, it can be difficult to pick it up again.

You Must Cross the Finish Line

Think of all those books you couldn't wait to read, but never actually finished. Reflect on the projects you started with the best of intentions, that petered into stagnation. How about the ideas that never moved into actual conception. Not everything is meant to be finished, but many of us have a boatload of projects, books, emails, and to-dos that have been relegated to a kind of purgatory of incompletion.

Completing unfinished tasks is a great way to change your life for the better. Unfinished tasks are huge silent stressors that steal hours of your precious time. They are energy and productivity thieves, but you can eliminate them.

From a button missing on your suit coat to the mess in your garage, every unfinished task is robbing you blind. Just like someone embezzling funds, these thieves don't steel in big obvious ways. They tug at your attention only for a few moments at a time. Not a big deal. Right? Wrong. Their cumulative effect is staggering. You may have as many as fifty unfinished tasks nagging at you.

Little Things Add Up

Some of these may only take a few moments of your attention. For example, a missing button is a moment of aggravation when you realize you still haven't sewn it on and then perhaps a few more minutes while you look for another outfit. A messy garage might mean a half an hour of frustration as you look for a misplaced tool. Not to mention the guilt you feel every time you walk through it and see the mess sitting there.

Just imagine if each of those fifty unfinished tasks took on the average only 30 seconds of your attention a day. Do you have any idea how much time you would needlessly lose a year? Try 9,125 minutes. That's approximately 152 hours, or almost four full forty hour work weeks.

What would your business look like if you had four extra weeks of creative attention, rather than distraction and stress? What would your relationships with you family and friends be like with an extra four weeks of attention?

So how do you stop these thieves? You do so with four simple steps.

Step by Step

Write down all of the unfinished task you can think of. Think about work and home and write down every disorganized drawer you have wanted to get to, project you keep thinking you will complete, appointment you have intended to set up. Write down tasks as small as sewing a button on to as big as an incomplete home renovation. Anything that isn't finished, write it down.

Just writing these tasks down will begin reducing the mental and emotional deficit they have been causing you. Congratulations, you're on your way!

Next to each unfinished task write down the first action step you must take to get moving. These action steps can be very small. For example, if you keep meaning to get your car into the shop because of some annoying rattle, then write down "call and setup appointment." If you want to store keepsakes in the attic, then write down "pick-up packing boxes on the way home from work."

You benefit from writing down the first step in two ways. First, procrastination is often times due to feeling overwhelmed, so focusing on the first step helps you overcome procrastination. Second, people who write down goals are tremendously more successful at accomplishing those goals than people who don't.

Complete the five easiest tasks first. Why? You have been stuck on this stuff forever. Half of the battle is just starting. Knocking out several easy tasks will help you over the mental hurdle that has been holding you back. Each success will add momentum. Dave Ramsey calls this snowballing. You gain momentum and enthusiasm as you complete each little task, picking up steam along the way. I like to think of it as small wins, eventually leading to a major victory.

Check off each completed task and immediately schedule the next action step you will take to complete another task. The biggest mistake people make after writing their list is shoving it to the side and never looking at it again. Avoid this mistake by using the completion of one task as a trigger for the next task.

The key is scheduling. Do not ever allow yourself the costly luxury of not having your next action scheduled. This is the defining difference between stressed-out people with wrinkled faces and peaceful people with completed lists.

You cannot imagine how much you will change your life for the better just by eliminating unfinished tasks until you do it. So don't hesitate. Start making you life better right now by creating your list of unfinished tasks and plow through it using these four simple tips.

QUALITY THE EXPERIENCE

"The difference between style and fashion is quality"
-Giorgio Armani

If you're like most gentlemen, then you have way too many clothes in your closet. If were really honest with ourselves, we probably realize that we have so many things that we haven't worn in years. Are you this way? I know that I was.

Everything changed when a friend and I engaged in a long conversation about scaling back and simplifying. My closet had grown out of control. I needed to takean honest and serious look at what I had and why. I'm sure there were some things in there that I really just didn't like and probably bought because they were on sale. I probably had things that I hadn't worn in over a year. Those things had to go.

The funny thing is when you start digging in your closet you truly realize how impulsive we can be as shoppers. So I made an effort to start reading blogs and websites dedicated to being a minimalist. Please note that I'm still not there yet, but I have decided to scale way back. There are many benefits of doing so.

Quality not Quantity

One of the most startling and sober and benefits is the realization that most people have quantity, not quality. What I learned is it's better to have more quality and less quantity. Instead of buying everything under the sun, I've given myself a theme or color scheme that I like to wear. This way my wardrobe is pretty much interchangeable.

It's easy to find an outfit or put a new combination together because most things match up easily. I wear a lot of blues and grays and I also wear a lot of white button-up shirts. When I want to add some color or have a little fun with patterns I can do so with my blazer, pocket square or tie.

I'm making sure these days that the quality of clothing surpasses the quantity. Let me assure you though this was not easy to do. I can recall staring into my closet, looking at all the clothes and shaking my head.

Too Much

Why did I have so much? But the real question was; did I need or even wear all of it? Sometimes as humans we get attached to having things. Yes, things. Some of us like shiny things, like jewelry. Some of us like expensive things, like electronics Most of all, a large majority of us like *a lot of things*. We simply have too much.

I forced myself to get out the trash bags and take a deep look at the excess. I was going to donate what I did not need. It was hard at first, pulling the shirts and pants off the hangers and stuffing them into the bags. It hurt even more when I did the same thing with the shoes that I did not wear on a regular basis.

In the end it afforded me a lot more space in my closet. My mother always says cluttered space cluttered mind and you know what she's right.

Now I have more space. Now I can easily see what I have. When I step out of the house now, I am more confident because I am sure that my shirts and pants are tailored perfectly. I know that I've been mentioning quality over quantity he when it comes to clothing, but this also applies in other aspects of your life.

Relationships

Your friends or your relationships sometimes need to be scaled back. From time to time, take a close look at them and examine them. There can sometimes be certain people or things that are cluttering up your mind. These things that need to be evaluated could even be bad habits. Just as I said, it wasn't easy to get rid of those unnecessary clothes, the same is true with habits. The effort will be worth it.

Start slowly as I did with my closet. Begin with small and incremental steps, analyzing what you truly need and what you do not need. Sometimes you will find that less is definitely more. You may need a close circle of friends and not an army of associates.

Make sure from time to time you are evaluating not just your closet but everything in your life. Scale back to keep only what is necessary or beneficial to making you a better person. Just as I did with my closet I found that I did not need as much as I had acquired. You may find the same thing to be true for you.

QUALITY THE PRINCIPLE

❦

"Quality means doing it right when no one is looking"
-Henry Ford

In our world, success is easily gauged by the things you own, your social standing, the jobs you hold, and how much money you make. There is nothing wrong with reaching for the stars and trying to reach your goals, but keep things in perspective. It's important, to remember that life isn't all about material possessions.

Give importance to the things that are truly lasting in life such as your family, friends. Find love and give love whenever and wherever you can. Give back to your community and help those in need. Build yourself to be the kind of person who finds satisfaction in doing more than just acquiring and building a good life for himself. Include others in your world.

Achieving Excellence

The people who have achieved tremendous amount of excellence in their life tend to be people who are excellent in one and only one aspect. Michael Jordan is a sports icon. Michael

Jordan has great athletic and kinesthetic ability. He also has a burning competitive desire to win and surpass his limits.

Although all sports require athleticism and a winning desire, Michael Jordan is only good in basketball. When he first retired in basketball in favor for baseball, he became an under performer. He was decent, but did not excel.

Michael Jordan can only achieve his greatness through basketball and not other sports. Sometimes we have to be the same way. We cannot always be an artist, a businessman and a fisherman. You may only be able to excel at one thing. That's totally fine. It is better to master one craft, than to be a Jack of all trades.

Time Management

It is always easier to concentrate, finish a task and move on as compared to trying to complete many different tasks at once. Humans by nature are not well-versed in the art of multi-tasking. You have probably experienced reading many emails while answering phone calls while drafting a proposal during your meal. Your outcome will turn out to be tedious and strenuous.

It's easier and more productive to tackle one project at a time. Take this book for instance. While writing it I had to focus most of my energy on the manuscript and lean on other members of the team to pick up the slack within the business structure. There's no shame in prioritizing.

Branding

People are brand sensitive. Ask any person what brand comes to their mind when sports shoes are being suggested, people will say Nike. When cool gadgets are being suggested, the brand Apple will come to their mind. What do Nike and Apple have in common? Both brands emphasize on premium quality. It is not a common product which is very affordable. People are raving fans of both brands. They'll overpay for the products. Why? Because of perceived quality.

Specialized Knowledge

It was once commonly said that knowledge is power. That is only a half-truth. When Henry Ford is being criticized for being uneducated and subsequently being challenged in court, he replied that he did not need to know the answers to the all the questions. He stated that all he needed was to gather his followers who have more knowledge than he posessed. But what we all need to be good at, is to be fantastic at managing people.

Time

Of all the resources we have at our disposal, time is the most finite. We can't make or buy more and we can't save it. We all get the exact same amount every single day. How do we apply the concept of "quality over quantity" to our time?

Think about how you spend it. It's fascinating how differently we each spend our equally allocated amount of minutes.

Some people seem to do so much more with their time, while others do remarkably less.

For myself, I have cut out a lot of unneccesary television watching and decided to focus that time on work projects. Later on, when I decide to relax or take a vacation, I can do so, however I like. You can put the time in up front and reap the benefits later.

But remember, this isn't about quantity or how much you can get done in a day. Being super productive is not necessarily the key to happiness. Sure, tearing through a long to-do list might give you a temporary sense of accomplishment and satisfaction. But is that enough for you? Is that happiness, or a short-lived high?

Choosing quality over quantity does not mean getting a lot done. What it does mean is spending as much of your time as possible doing what makes you happy. There are two ways to accomplish this.

Be a Well Oiled Machine

Be more efficient. By more quickly completing tasks you don't love, you'll have more time left to spend doing things you truly enjoy. Imagine also doing less of the things you don't love.

In today's world there is so much pressure to succeed and to have the right look. We often times do end up comprising our view on quality versus quantity. I want you to know that feeling this pressure is absolutely normal but you must find a happy medium between what is right for you and what will help you succeed.

We do have to achieve certain things in our lives, but we must also pay attention to how we get there. The journey is just as important, if not more important, as the destination. Your life is your own. Live it as you want to live it and be proud of it.

Honor the gift of life. There is more to life than acquiring and having material things. Find out what makes life more meaningful for you. That is truly living a life filled with quantity.

POSITIVITY THE EXPERIENCE

❧

"Your positive action combined with positive thinking results in success"

-Shiv Khera

If you could see me right now as I'm working on this book, you might shake your head and laugh. Right now my arm is in a sling and it's very difficult for me to move the left side of my upper body. As I stated in the outset of this book, I decided to step out of my comfort zone and get my motorcycle license. I was taking a motorcycle certification course when out of nowhere the unexpected happened. Performing a routine training exercise, I was riding along, slightly too fast, making a left-hand turn and when I went down.

I would like to say it was because of the pouring down rain that was going on during the class. Why we didn't postpone the class due to the very heavy rain I'll never know. But hey, I signed the waiver. I also have to be honest with myself and realize that I was very inexperienced.

There I was trying to learn something new and step out of my comfort zone and the next minute I'm laying on the ground with the motorcycle pretty much on top of me. The good thing is that I wore a helmet.

As I hopped up and shook myself off I realized right then something was wrong. I wasn't quite sure what it was but something was off. My arm and my shoulder kind of made a popping noise when I moved it. But I didn't feel terribly bad...yet.

Pain Before Joy

Perhaps it was the adrenaline searching through my body that propelled me to keep going. I almost was ready to get back in line and take my turn on the exercise again. But the nagging pain in my left shoulder would not go away. One of the instructors insisted that we call the paramedics to have a closer look at my shoulder.

When they arrived on the scene and assessed the injury they insisted that I needed to come with them. So I was placed into an ambulance and taken to a hospital which was literally one block away. Once situated in the hospital the pain started to set in and I knew something was seriously wrong.

I'd gone my whole life without breaking so much as a finger or toe and now I was thinking in my head that I broke something. I was also praying that just maybe it would just be a bad bruise or a dislocation and they could "pop it back in."

Boy was I wrong. Once I made it to the x-ray technician they were almost certain that something serious was going on. Next they wanted to do a CAT scan, which made me super nervous.

Waiting Game

I sat alone, staring at the ceiling, waiting for the doctor to come in with the diagnosis. I kept thinking about different scenarios going through my head. Your mind starts to drift and I imagined words like surgery or even amputation. When the doctor did come in I instantly knew it was serious.

They informed me that I had a broken scapula. Meaning my left shoulder blade had been broken at three different places. Leave it to me to do this. Less than 1% of all fractures are to the scapula. Meaning, it's really hard to break. That wasn't enough for me. I also had broken one of my ribs. Everyone who has seen me since the accident has asked the same question. Is my motorcycle career over? In short, probably, yes.

Let's just say I'm a quick learner. That doesn't mean that I learned to ride very quickly. Obviously. What it means is that I can understand when something is not for me. I can take a hint. It's just a shame that it took a broken scapula for me to find out I was not the next Evil Knievel.

Once I'd received my diagnosis I was told that I would need to follow up with a specialist within a few days. By the time I was discharged, the pharmacy was closed and all I was given was a hearty handshake and a prescription to fill the next day. I had been in the hospital for about five hours in soaking wet clothes. Talk about feeling defeated. This was one of the times in life when I wanted to hang my head and kick myself for trying something new.

Thinking it Over

Who did I think I was? Why was I ready to buy a motorcycle? What made me think I was going to be successful at learning that new skill? As it turned out I failed the class. I guess I didn't even need to tell you that part. Why am I telling you this story?

I'm telling you this story because one week after that incident I'm diving in and writing this book. Instead of sitting on the couch binge watching Netflix or watching College Football from noon to midnight, I'm doing something positive. I decided to take those lemons I was given and turn it in to ice cold lemonade.

I have the time on my hands and I'm going to put it to good use. You're probably wondering how I'm typing with one hand. Here's the secret. I'm not. Once again I dove in and started doing research and so I am using a dictation system to record my voice and therefore the computer is typing for me.

I know that this will be my most successful book to date. Why do I say that? Because I'm more dedicated and more driven than ever. I know that just because something bad happened, that doesn't mean life is going to stay that way. I look at the positives in life now.

That accident really gave me the kick in the pants to get my writing into high gear. I've been thinking about writing again for quite some time. Thanks to that accident I'm doing it.

Stay Positive

I hope the lessons and the stories that I'm sharing as well as the information that is in these pages is helping to assist you in your life. Many people have faced many situations much worse than my motorcycle accident. In fact, I truly realize how fortunate I am. I have had the support of my friends and family every step of the way. My parents have come over to assist me and my wife and my children have been very accommodating.

All of us have to look at the bright side. We have to be grateful for the things that we do have. In fact, I went out to breakfast before writing this. I went to a hometown diner with my wife and I saw a man leaving the restaurant. He held open the door for us and I noticed that he was missing his left hand. That brought everything into perspective. Perfect clarity. I gave that gentleman a nod and a thank you. I looked down at my arm, grateful, knowing it would heal.

I had a doctor appointment earlier in the week and found out I'm on track for 100% recovery. There is no reason for me or you not to live with positivity. What has happened to you that gets you down? What has been your motorcycle accident? What problems are you facing? There is no problem so large that you cannot overcome it. You just have to stay positive.

Think about all the things that are going in your favor. Just the fact that you can read this book or listen to this book on audio is a blessing.

Remember that you woke up this morning and you got out of bed. These are true miracles. There are so many people around the world that would love to trade places with you. Maybe you're experiencing financial hardship. Maybe you are having problems in a personal relationship. It doesn't matter because you have the opportunity to change those things to make them better.

Think about someone who is stuck in a situation where they really can't change. Perhaps there is a man or woman in a underdeveloped country that is wondering when their next meal is going to come from. There are children that don't know how they will get clean water to drink.

Those are serious concerns. I know that we all have problems but we have to look at it in the grand scheme of things and if we stay positive we will overcome our situation. By staying negative our brain will stop working and looking for solutions. By staying positive we will be optimistic and be searching for answers and solutions to our problems.

I hope that you find the encouragement you are looking for in this book. I am 100% sure that I do not have all the answers. All I can do is use my experiences to encourage you to have a positive outlook and know that you too can have a bright future. Let's look at some practical ways in which we can instill positivity into our life to make a change for the greater good.

POSITIVITY THE PRINCIPLE

"I think if you just look at life in a positive way, positive things will happen"

-Jake Owen

Have you ever noticed that, when you are playing and doing what you love and are passionate about, that the task or activity feels effortless and so much easier to engage in than an activity you don't love so much? It may seem that these activities are easier to do and time seems to fly by.

Your attitude is much more positive and you feel more relaxed. You tend not to think about what you are doing or how you are doing it. You just, well, do it. This is also a time where you feel great about yourself in every aspect of life and nothing else in the world matters.

When you are doing something you love, enjoy and are passionate about, your mind is in a state where frustration, fear, and anxiety is no longer present. You no doubt feel free from those shackles of the expected. Your mind naturally falls into a state of creativity that is genuine and it shows in your attitude. You become full of life!

When you are engaging in activities or tasks that are not preferred, expected or demanded of you it feels like more of a job. When you are not truly engaged in the task, your mindset changes. Your attitude and frame of mind goes from positive to negative. This is where your mind is at its lowest. This is a danger zone.

Issues

When problems arise you may feel like you are suffering by being put through the absolute worst kind of torture imaginable. When you go from play to this lower state of mind you begin to naturally show resistance towards yourself and your obligations in life and towards others.

In short, you become negative. At this point, people are not drawn to you. Your energy level drops low. How can you turn it all around?

Create the Change

The state of creating is a mindset where you are feeling good about yourself, your productivity increases as does your intuition. When in this mindset, you use all the energy you have to create these positive feelings and outcomes for yourself.

Your creativity can come out in various forms. You can try writing, taking risks, trying new things, painting, or other activities. This will also show as a person working in the business world as it will help you become more creative in your presentation techniques, speaking with potential and current customers, and developing new and innovative marketing strategies.

Remember, being in this creative mindset is a positive way to think. You will know when you are in this mindset because you will begin to feel a sense of joy and tedious tasks will not feel so tedious. An inspirational feeling will come over you and you'll feel a sense of empowerment.

You may even notice a certain spark or internal push to get those tasks done with little effort, without over-thinking the task at hand. In turn, you will feel less resistance to completing those tasks. The most important thing to remember is to let go of the resistance.

Mindset Development

If you are living in this positive mindset, resistance to completing tasks or engaging in certain activities will disappear. This will result in leaving you feeling less frustrated, less fatigued, energized, and excited about taking on new challenges and following through with those challenges.

One of the key components to being in this creative mindset is that you are not aiming for a specific outcome. If something does not work with the task you are working on, you accept that and immediately begin to make changes to correct the mistakes.

You can adapt to the quick changes of the situation and continue working on the task as you were. Again, there is no sense of failure in this positive mindset. Through each mistake you make, you take that in, run with it and continue to improve.

Learn from those mistakes and let them help you evolve.

The eventual unintentional outcome is the mastering all aspects of this task or activity until you are the best at taking on and completing this task in your field of work. All of the effort you put forth to making those tasks and activities work including making adaptations and coming up with new solutions will bring a sense of fulfillment. You will experience excitement, pride, and most importantly happiness.

You may feel unstoppable and your elation will move you to want to share your products and services with the world because you now know that many people will benefit from them. This is because you decided to take action to improve the situation rather than focus on the fact that you failed.

You're Ready

Once you have reached this state of acceptance, your core abilities will naturally resonate from you and will be effortless. You will be able to think clearly, your self-esteem will improve. You will be able to express yourself more positively, allowing others to see the positive mindset you are in.

You will be able to express your feelings openly without resistance or hesitation. Your intuition and creativity will become sharper and more prevalent as you'll be able to connect with others effortlessly and comfortably.

Over-thinking can stop anyone in their tracks. You begin to obsess over things that are non-essential or that you have no control over. Remember, again, not to fall into this trap.

Thinking about making a change and actually doing it are two different things. The only way to take back control of your negative thoughts is to take action.

When your mindset is in this creative state of mind, your mind is relaxed and blank. This will help you achieve effectiveness in the actions you take to fix a situation. Don't think. Just act!

If you often find yourself constantly searching for new ideas and struggling with coming up with a plan to change things, you immediately put yourself in a negative mindset. When people are constantly telling you that your ideas are not possible or you can't get it done, don't fret.

It is important to keep your composure and not to take these criticisms personal. Many higher-ups in large companies have done the same things consistently for several years he or she may be resistant to the change.

Have you worked for a company who does the same thing that they've been doing for years? They do these same things, because that's the way they have always been done. Do not allow yourself to fall into their trap.

We never want to allow other people's resistance to change force us into a state of resistance. You will become frustrated and will begin to question your own capabilities in your position.

Remember, being in and staying in the creative mindset will continue to feed that positive energy and it is that energy that drives improvement and change. Only those people who are in the mindset of fear of change can stop change.

Continue to Learn

Results will only happen if you are willing to adapt and change your way of thinking. Once you have mastered this you will be able to learn so much more about your own capabilities and where to improve.

Use learning to walk as an example. As a toddler learning to walk, you probably took several falls but yet got right back up and tackled the challenge. This is a natural reaction for a toddler. First you learn to crawl, then walk, then eventually run. This same concept can be applied to the real world.

You may be presenting change to someone and you get knocked down. Don't allow yourself to stay down. Get right back up and start pushing for change again. That is the mindset you need to be in to maximize your productivity and continuously improve yourself.

Life is a learning process. You will always be learning regardless of how old you are. When you stop learning and growing life becomes dull. We don't want a dull life. We want a vibrant life.

GENEROSITY THE EXPERIENCE

"Generosity is giving more than you can, and pride is taking less than you need"

– Khalil Gibran

Last summer my family and I took a weekend trip to Chicago, Illinois. We really enjoy that city and always have a nice time when we visit there. I like to stay right downtown on Michigan Avenue or as close as possible to the famous Magnificent Mile. On that particular trip we had done most of the tourist things like Navy Pier and the Children's Museum and we decided to do some shopping. As we split up my daughter went with my wife and my son stayed with me.

My son is finally the age where he starting to understand the world around him a little bit more. He's also still at the age where he has to go to the bathroom immediately or else it becomes some sort of national crisis.

The Zara store we were shopping in had many floors. Once on the third floor, my little guy decides he has to go. I approached the sales clerk and asked for directions to the restroom. Of course, it was out of order. So there we were frantically hurdling down three flights of escalators, pushing through a crowd and spilling out onto the packed sidewalk.

Searching and Noticing

I had to find this kid a restroom. There were so many people on the sidewalks and I was scanning buildings, looking for somewhere for him to go. Of course the nearby hotels don't have restrooms in the lobby, because of all the homeless people downtown. They don't want homeless people coming in using the restroom, scaring off customers or just hanging out. I'm not saying it's right or wrong it's just the way it is there. I finally found a restaurant that had a bathroom in it, so we went in.

After taking care of necessities, we decided to get a little snack. I knew that within a matter of minutes he was going to tell me how hungry he was. That's just the way it is when you have kids. They are either hungry or thirsty or have to go to the bathroom. I try to stay one step ahead of them so I got us a little bit of food. Well, I ordered the food and then I thought to myself, here is a teachable moment. I decided to order a little bit of extra food.

We took the food to go and headed outside. Once we got outside we immediately noticed the many homeless people that were around. It's sad that sometimes people don't even notice the homeless population but they're there. The homeless are usually in the corners, sifting through a garbage can looking for a meal at all times.

Back in our home community it's rare to see homeless wandering the streets. Sure, we have panhandlers with signs at stoplights asking for help or saying they will work for food, but it's not like downtown Chicago or other metropolitan cities. In many crowded areas the homeless are rampant and in your face.

Small Gesture

I saw a man sitting alone and off to the side. I had actually spotted him on our way in. He was looking in trash can apparently for soda cans or for food. I wasn't sure what he was searching for, but I knew he was in need. When we came out of the restaurant he was still there looking very dejected.

My son and I were not too far away, eating our food when my son asked me a question. "Dad, why does he look so angry?" he asked, nodding his baseball cap towards the homeless man. I told him that he wasn't angry, just frustrated.

My son then asked the next logical question. "Why?" I told him because he was probably hungry and didn't have anywhere to sleep tonight.

I do my best to remind my children how fortunate we are to have food, clothing, and adequate shelter. I let them know that there are others that do not have these basic necessities. But still it's hard to get these concepts into the mind of a six-year-old child.

My son kept looking over towards the man. He seemed bothered about something. Being an inquisitive youngster my son asked me why no one gives the man food or money. I also explained that everyone is busy trying to survive themselves and sometimes they forget to reach back and help others. But at this moment I told him we could do something right now to change things for that man today. It would not change his life, but it could make a small difference and sometimes the smallest difference is all it takes to turn the situation around.

I cautiously started to approach the man. I could tell my son was somewhat nervous to go with me, so I let him stay back behind me just a bit. I said a hello to the man and asked him if he would like to have a meal. I told him it wasn't much, but hopefully it would be something that would help him out. The man was happy to accept. He slowly reached out his hand as I placed a brown carryout bag into his outstretched fingers. The man mumbled a thank you and I wished him a good day.

As we walked away I assured my son that the man appreciated our little gesture. He looked up at me and agreed, stating that he was glad the man wouldn't be hungry for lunch. I let him know that dinner would present another struggle for the man but that we had at least done something to help.

Little Things

I know in the big scheme of things it was probably an insignificant gesture, a drop in the bucket as it were. Homelessness is a huge problem in our country and it's not going to be fixed by passing out small take out bags in major metropolitan cities. The idea was to show my son that generosity, even in the smallest form has a place in the life of every gentleman. It is in our best interest to give if we are in a position to give.

If we can donate to causes that we believe in, let us donate. If we can give back our time or resources, let's give back in abundance. We can be generous with family members and our friends. It does not always have to be monetary giving. Generosity can be shown by lending a hand in so many different ways.

I hope that you remember that you can make an impact on someone else's life. It may not seem like a large gesture to you, but to someone else it could be just the thing that ignites a fire in them and shows them that people still care it can give people hope.

What talents or abilities can you lend? Is there any possible way that you can donate or give back to a charity or cause of your choice? You will definitely feel satisfaction and fulfillment by doing so. By extending yourself to the degree possible you are showing that you are a caring individual. You will be signifying that you not only want to better your life, but you want to better the lives of others.

Simply put, being generous is a telling sign that you have acquired the mind of a gentleman. The wisest man to ever walk the earth said that there is more happiness in giving than receiving. How true those words are! Let's look more into generosity and the benefits of giving.

GENEROSITY THE PRINCIPLE

❦

"There is overwhelming evidence that the higher the level of self-esteem, the more likely one will be to treat others with respect, kindness, and generosity"

– Nathaniel Branden

Throughout most cultures and societies generosity has been and still is considered as a positive quality of human character. Even people who are not or do not regard themselves as generous, if honest enough would often admit to admire and appreciate this trait in other people.

Going beyond the purely historic and traditional perception of generosity as a virtue which many people take for granted, it might be interesting to think how this gesture is useful not only to the recipient of generosity, but to the one who actually shows generosity.

In the present context, generosity will be defined in a more general way as the act or attitude of giving. This is because generosity is not only a materialistic or financial expression. Generosity is rather an attitude of being ready and willing to give without demanding or expecting something in return.

Imagine a simple situation where you are having a morning café in the neighborhood and there is a person sitting alone on a nearby table with a sad face. You do not know anything about that person and you do not have any personal attraction, interest or curiosity about him.

You have no personal reason whatsoever. Just because he happens to be sad and you happen to be there, you take the step to join him and try to cheer him up. Generosity might be as simple as that.

It's Worth It

Going back to the subject of benefits it might seem that there is contradiction. On one hand we defined generosity as giving without demand or expectations, but on the other hand we talk about generosity being beneficial to the one who gives. How do we reconcile those two ideas? The answer to this question relates to our psyche. What is the necessary prerequisite of giving?

First of all, you cannot give something which you feel that you do not have. Secondly, you can afford to give only that for which you feel you have enough. Further on, what is the definition of enough? Enough can mean different things to different people. The definition is completely subjective and can be specified only in the context of the individual perception.

The more you give, the better you feel. There is something about being generous that actually improves your own quality of life. There is really no need to hold back.

Some traditional teachings and also new-age gurus talk about the Law of attraction, where you get what you give out.

By being generous, generosity will flow back to you. Being kind to others reaps the result of others being kind to you.

However, such metaphysical statements may sound trendy, but there is actually a more psychological point of view.

The subjective feeling of abundance which you actively train by being generous will help you be more at peace with yourself in general, because our personal experience that we call life is nothing but a subjective perception of a reality that only seems to be outwardly objective.

It Works

Studies have consistently showed that an act of generosity that generates good, positive emotions creates the most benefits, not just to the giver but also to the recipient and society.

Being charitable is good for the giver in terms of both body and mind. Acts of generosity and kindness enhance your physical health by strengthening your immune system, reducing the risk of cardiac events and increasing your lifespan.

People who are generous are also likely to have healthier psychological well-being. They have a greater sense of self worth, self confidence and sense of purpose in life. They are also generally happier. Generous people are less prone to anxiety and depression.

According to Barbara Frederickson, they tend to have more positive emotions and therefore more likely to flourish with greater creativity and productivity. They are also more resilience, coping better with challenges and obstacles. Is that enough reasons to be generous for you? I hope so.

People who are at the receiving end of generosity get what they needed or wanted. They feel a sense of gratitude, which is another positive emotion - and a greater trust in humanity.

The act of generosity enriches humanity as a whole. It spreads good feelings all around, leading to more similar acts of kindness from others. In this way, it also promotes harmony, peace and joy. It enhances our trust in humanity. In short, it betters us.

Additional Benefits

Generosity is one of the most admired characteristics anyone can express. Think about the business man who donates large amounts to charity, or the child who gives his hard-earned allowance to a disaster relief, or the elderly woman who freely gives a portion of what little food she has to a food drive. We appreciate and admire their generous giving. These stories are heartwarming and inspire us.

However, appreciation and admiration are not the only benefits of generosity. A generous person will experience heartfelt joy when they help meet the needs of others. They will be happier and find that just as they refresh others, they too are refreshed. Their own needs will be abundantly supplied for.

What about those who are not generous? Well the same proverb previously mentioned says they will fall into poverty. This could be financial or material poverty, or emotional poverty. Those that are greedy tend to never be satisfied with what they have and continually need more.

Why not choose to develop your generous side? Generosity begins in the heart and is expressed through action. Extending generosity to others is a win-win situation. As you willingly give to others, watch as your own needs are abundantly supplied for in life.

With all the evidence pointing to the many benefits of generosity, it is now up to us to incorporate it into our daily lives and enhance our own happiness and personal growth.

CONCLUSION

∞

As you look back over these ten principles, you'll find that each of them is different, yet connected to one another. This is important to remember, because there are many aspects of our life that combine to make us a whole person. By working on these principles and applying them on a daily basis you will start to see life changes. This will be a gradual, but steady change for the good.

Adapting the mindset of a gentleman is not neccesarily an easy task. If it were the world would be filled with gentlemen that are focused and driven. Sadly, this is not what we see when we look around the world today. Being a true gentleman is like being part of an elite club. The benefits of membership are worth your effort.

Soon you will find that you are living with more confidence and earning the respect of others. Keep in mind that the goal is not to only receive praise from others but to inspire others. We don't do things to impress others, but rather to impress upon them that we are respectful, responsible and productive members of society.

Developing the mindset of a gentleman is sure to help you reach your set goals and achieve what you set your mind to.

Self doubt, procrastination and self pity will become things of the past. Your mind will see the opportunities in front of you and help you recall how blessed you are to be in this game called life.

We all have a decision to make each day when we rise out of bed. I hope that you have affirmed it in your mind to act, live and think like a gentleman.

www.ingramcontent.com/pod-product-compliance
Lightning Source LLC
Chambersburg PA
CBHW061748020426
42331CB00006B/1394